My School Scavenger Hunt

Bela Davis

Abdo Kids Junior
is an Imprint of Abdo Kids
abdobooks.com

Abdo

SENSES SCAVENGER HUNT

Kids

abdobooks.com

Published by Abdo Kids, a division of ABDO, P.O. Box 398166, Minneapolis, Minnesota 55439.
Copyright © 2023 by Abdo Consulting Group, Inc. International copyrights reserved in all countries.
No part of this book may be reproduced in any form without written permission from the publisher.
Abdo Kids Junior™ is a trademark and logo of Abdo Kids.

Printed in the United States of America, North Mankato, Minnesota.

052022

092022

THIS BOOK CONTAINS
RECYCLED MATERIALS

Photo Credits: Getty Images, Shutterstock

Production Contributors: Teddy Borth, Jennie Forsberg, Grace Hansen

Design Contributors: Candice Keimig, Pakou Moua

Library of Congress Control Number: 2021950712

Publisher's Cataloging-in-Publication Data

Names: Davis, Bela, author.

Title: My school scavenger hunt / by Bela Davis.

Description: Minneapolis, Minnesota : Abdo Kids, 2023 | Series: Senses scavenger hunt | Includes online
    resources and index.

Identifiers: ISBN 9781098261566 (lib. bdg.) | ISBN 9781644948378 (pbk.) | ISBN 9781098262402
    (ebook) | ISBN 9781098262822 (Read-to-Me ebook)

Subjects: LCSH: Senses and sensation--Juvenile literature. | Schools--Juvenile literature. | Scavenger
    hunting--Juvenile literature.

Classification: DDC 612.8--dc23

Table of Contents

School Scavenger Hunt

Let's go on a hunt! Can we find these things in a school?

1 the word "school"
- - - - - - - - - - - - - - - -

 2 cold locker
- - - - - - - - - - - - - - - -

3 reading aloud
- - - - - - - - - - - - - - - -

 4 art class smell
- - - - - - - - - - - - - - - -

 5 bread taste
- - - - - - - - - - - - - - - -

6 instrument sound
- - - - - - - - - - - - - - - -

We have five **senses**. They can help find things.

I see with my eye.

I see a school bus.

I feel with my hand.

I feel a cold locker.

I hear with my ear. I hear
a teacher reading.

I smell with my nose.

I smell paint.

I taste with my tongue.

I taste a sandwich.

I hear with my ear.

I hear a **flute**.

We found all 6 things!
Can you find them in your
school? Happy hunting!

Make Your Own Scavenger Hunt

Decide Where to Go

Make a List of Things You May Find

Add Senses to That List

Find Your Things!